Vlogging

A Complete Beginner's Guide to Vlogging

(How to Use the Power of Video to Successfully Grow Your Online Following and Make a Profit)

Anthony Russell

Published By **Bella Frost**

Anthony Russell

All Rights Reserved

Vlogging : A Complete Beginner's Guide to Vlogging (How to Use the Power of Video to Successfully Grow Your Online Following and Make a Profit)

ISBN   978-1-998901-85-2

Legal & Disclaimer

The information contained in this book is not designed to replace or take the place of any form of medicine or professional medical advice. The information in this book has been provided for educational & entertainment purposes only.

The information contained in this book has been compiled from sources deemed reliable, and it is accurate to the best of the Author's knowledge; however, the Author cannot guarantee its accuracy and validity and cannot be held liable for any errors or omissions. Changes are periodically made to this book. You must consult your doctor or get professional medical advice before using any of the suggested remedies, techniques, or information in this book.

Upon using the information contained in this book, you agree to hold harmless the Author

TABLE OF CONTENTS

Introduction

Vlogging is ending up being progressively more prominent and there has actually never ever been a greater time to begin a vlog. Individuals truly delight in viewing top quality vlogs and certain vloggers have millions of subscribers. However, you do not require countless subscribers to generate income from vlogging. There are lots of vloggers who have a good deal less subscribers which make full-time earnings and more from their vlogging endeavors. What might be better? Doing something that you like and capturing it to show the world and generating income simultaneously. This is more than a dream-- it could be your truth if you adhere to the recommendations offered within this guide.

Within this book, you are going to find what a vlog truly is, some terrific and lucrative ideas for beginning a vlog, how to begin your brand-new vlog with optimal impact and how to advertise your vlog so that you boost your subscriber count and your capacity to generate income.

I have actually responded to all of the most typical concerns about vlogging within this guide and supplied you with a step by step strategy to produce an effective and successful vlog. You have to act and be absolutely devoted to your brand-new vlog. It will require some time and work to get where you wish to be.

I have actually left no stone unturned within this book. You are going to understand precisely what is expected of you and the ins and outs of vlogging. Consistency is all when it comes to vlogging as you are going to uncover as you go through this book.

As soon as you have actually checked out the guide, you are going to have all that you require to begin your journey to effective vlogging. So I suggest that you read this book completely first and after that return to the beginning and follow the advised action steps.

Chapter 1: What is Vlogging

A video blog (vlog) or "vlogging" is the establishing of a particular channel on a video sharing website like YouTube and submitting videos regularly. The objective of your vlog is to supply appealing material in a particular niche which is going to produce a response from viewers and expand your subscriber base or following. Vlogging blasted off around 10 years back when video sharing websites such as YouTube ended up being truly popular. Videos are a great deal more fascinating than text-based material. Many folks would sooner view a brief video than check out numerous words of text.

Could vlogging actually make you cash? Yes, it definitely can, however, you have to handle it in the proper way, which is what this manual is all about. You are going to see how to select a specific niche to vlog about, the most effective video platform to utilize, how to establish your channel properly and a whole lot more.

Why Should You Start a Vlog?

There are lots of excellent reasons why you ought to begin a vlog today. The very first of these is that video has a significant impact nowadays. Facebook and YouTube presently control the world of Web video. There is a reason why both of these networks launched live streaming video-- it is what individuals desire! Individuals like to see videos and specifically, they like vlogs. A few of the most prosperous channels on YouTube are vlogs. When you begin to get a following for your vlog, the word is going to spread rapidly and you are going to get a great deal more subscribers.

Vlogging is among the ideal methods for you to share your skills, thoughts and ideas about a topic. When you develop a vlog your audience is not expecting Hollywood film quality-- actually, quite the opposite. A vlog has to be genuine and informal and truly relate to the audience.

There are all sorts of effective vlogs available. A great deal of travel vlogs make it possible for the vloggers to travel around the globe through contributions, sponsorship, affiliate marketing and various other income possibilities. Have a look at the appeal of reality TV-- individuals like to see other regular folks doing things that they enjoy.

In case you have a particular skill, then you can demonstrate to the world how you put this to excellent use. As soon as you begin to develop a following, then there are going to be possibilities for you to market your abilities. By showing that you are actually proficient at something in your vlog, you are bound to get demands from individuals thinking about hiring you.

Certain individuals begin a vlog since they wish to record their life and develop a memory to show future generations. They have no monetary goals for doing so. This is a book about generating income from vlogging, so I would not suggest this technique. Nevertheless, a variety of vloggers who began by doing this have actually made passive income.

There are currently some really prosperous vloggers on YouTube who earn a substantial profit from their vlog. Individuals such as Lilly Singh, Roman Attwood, Zoella, Casey Neistat, and Alfie Deyes are all fine examples.

These individuals all have deals with brand names where they earn a considerable profit. Brands continuously search

YouTube for brand-new vloggers and in case they discover good ones, they are going to approach them straight with offers or sponsorship. There are numerous possibilities to generate income with vlogging.

You could begin vlogging today. There is no requirement for you to acquire costly camera equipment initially. If you have a mobile phone that could capture top-quality video, then you are good to go. Nevertheless, in case you can buy great recording devices, I would usually advise this.

When you have actually wrapped up shooting your video footage, you could then transfer this to your computer system and utilize cost-free video editing software like Windows Movie Maker for Windows devices or iMovie for Mac. Yes, there are superior video editors available, however, you do not require them to get going.

You do not even require a site. Utilize YouTube as your vlogging platform. It is a great idea to have social profiles like Facebook, Twitter and Instagram and construct a following on these so that you could allow everybody to know when you have actually released a fresh video.

A variety of vloggers utilize affiliate marketing to produce revenue. For instance, there are a variety of effective makeup and cosmetics vlogs and the owners advertise items and earn commissions as an affiliate.

What Should your Vlog Be About ?

The primary guideline with developing a vlog is to make it about anything which you are truly intrigued by. There are no set guidelines here-- you can actually develop a vlog about anything. However, I would recommend that you comply with the actions listed beneath to recognize a truly excellent vlogging topic:

1. Compose a list of the things which truly intrigue you in life. Incorporate everything here like things which you delight in doing at work, in your free time, with your buddies, and so on.

2. Compose a second list of the skills that you possess. Do not even believe that you have no skills-- you are going to be proficient at some things for certain.

3. Take a look at these lists and consider the business possibilities with each interest and skill. In case you are a sports fan, for instance, and follow a specific team, in that case, is there an opportunity

available for you? Certain sports vlog owners are rich!

4. Utilize the Google Keyword Planner to assess and see the number of searches per month that exist for your passions and skills. You could likewise browse on YouTube to see which videos show up and the number of subscribers and views they have.

5. Select your vlogging subject based upon the most effective blend of interest or skills and business possibilities. The majority of vlogging guides are going to inform you to simply vlog about something which you are passionate about. You are going to definitely want to be enthusiastic about your vlogging, yet not all topics have the very same lucrative potential.

6. As soon as you have actually picked a vlogging topic or niche, you are going to

have to assess to see if you can produce lots of videos with it. Individuals are going to want you to vlog typically-- you can't simply submit one video and expect wonders. So is there ample material for you to develop a weekly or month-to-month vlog? In the following chapter, you are going to discover some terrific ideas for beginning a rewarding vlog.

The Benefits of Starting a Vlog

There are a variety of benefits of a vlog over a basic blog site. The primary reason because of which individuals choose to produce basic blog sites is that it is much easier than producing a vlog. You could compose a post for a basic blog site relatively quickly or outsource it to an expert writer. However, it is unsurprising that individuals choose video.

With a basic blog site it is really challenging to establish a following. Ranking blog sites in the search engines is truly hard nowadays, and there are individuals promoting various blog sites all across social networks. The competition is harsh. Indeed there is competition in vlogging, however, it is a lot less extreme.

- Individuals Vlog for more visibility-- it is simpler to get visitors to a vlog than it is to a basic blog site.

- Videos have a better chance of going viral-- you have a lot better odds of one of your vlog videos going viral than a basic article.

- Videos are more involved-- it is simpler to encourage individuals to do something with a video than it is with a composed article. You are going to be a lot more probable to attain greater conversion rates with excellent videos.

- Video Tutorials are truly powerful--individuals like to understand how to do particular things. In case you can demonstrate to them how to attain something with a video tutorial, then this is even more fascinating than them needing to read a lengthy article with screenshots.

- You can Vlog Live-- with the live streaming functionalities of Facebook and YouTube, you can produce some videos live. In case you have an essential statement to make, then inform individuals that there will be a live stream on a particular day and at a specific time. Individuals actually enjoy live-streaming video!

- There are a variety of revenue-generating options-- from the YouTube Partnership Program to sponsorship, exclusive deals with brand names and affiliate marketing. Prominent vlogs have numerous choices when it concerns generating income.

You want to be truly dedicated to your vlog. If you invest a couple of months adding videos to your channel and after that quit, for a while, individuals are going to forget you quickly. This suggests that you are going to have lost time and work for nothing.

In case you select a topic for vlogging and there are various vloggers on YouTube in the equivalent niche, then don't allow this to put you off. Keep in mind that you are the topic of your vlog. You are different from other vloggers with your distinct individuality.

Chapter 2: Ideas for Successful Vlogs

It could be hard to come up with that winning idea for a vlog which is going to make you substantial revenue. So to assist you, here are some excellent ideas for you within this chapter. I hope that you discover an idea here which you are able to run with.

Video Games

Are you somebody who takes pleasure in playing video games a great deal? There are numerous individuals who play video games nowadays, and there is constantly space for another fantastic vlog on the topic. New video games show up constantly, and with the increase in appeal of Amazon's Twitch.tv there is a lot of potential for you to develop excellent videos. The trick to an effective video game vlog is supplying the video gaming community with what they desire. If they delight in the videos you produce, then they are going to get the word out for you and your vlog is going to grow tremendously. Here are a few ideas for videos you can produce:

- You playing a particular video game and beating a level or defeating a boss.

- A live stream regarding a specific video game

- A review of a video game.

- Your top 10 video games.

- Develop a video game walkthrough.

- Offer video gaming news.

Tutorials or How-To Videos

A great deal of individuals browse YouTube to discover how to perform something. So do you have a specific set of abilities or are you a pro in a specific topic? If so, a series of "how-to" videos might be an excellent vlogging idea for you. Individuals are constantly utilizing the Web to pose questions, and videos are by far the most prominent medium which individuals select to get the responses which they require. There are simply limitless possibilities for " how-to" video tutorials. You could certainly advertise affiliate items or offer your own items on the back of a vlog this way. Here are a few ideas:

- How to construct something.

- How to generate income online.

- Life abilities.

- Personal growth abilities.

- How to get a girlfriend/boyfriend and subsequent relationship tips.

- Discover a brand-new language.

- How to secure that brand-new job and maintain it.

- How to generate income in stocks, forex and so on.

Computer systems and Technology

Do you like computer systems and tech devices? Are you an expert on mobile phones? There are a lot of individuals that simply like computer systems and tech and would be thrilled to discover what is ensuing and so on. The world of innovation alters constantly, so you are never going to ever lack video ideas. Here are several great ideas:

- Beneficial apps for your mobile phone.

- The most effective laptop computers.

- How to utilize prominent software applications like Microsoft Office.

- Fresh technology reviews.

- Technology item comparisons.

- Computer system hacks and unfamiliar shortcuts.

- Create your personal site.

- Registering a domain name.

- How to make your computer system quicker.

- How to repair typical computer issues.

Weight Loss and Fitness

Do you have an understanding about how to slim down and maintain the weight off? Are you a fitness pro? The need for "how-to" videos within this area is big. And the topic is so huge that you ought to never ever lack new video ideas. Here are several ideas to consider:

- Weight loss pointers

- Compare prominent diet plans e.g. Paleo, Keto and so on

- Healthy dietary dishes.

- How to stay away from food and drinks which are going to make you put on weight.

- Working out for novices.

- How to perform a workout appropriately e.g. push-ups.

- How to get in shape and shredded without heading to the fitness center.

- The advantages of yoga.

- Particular yoga workouts.

Personal Growth

This is another big topic. Individuals constantly wish to enrich their lives and in case you have the understanding to aid them to accomplish this, then it can unlock all types of doors. Here are several terrific video ideas:

- X ways to be more positive.

- How to conquer your worries.

- How to get out of your comfort zone.

- How to establish goals and accomplish them.

- How to boost your self-confidence.

- How to be a terrific communicator.

- How to encourage individuals to perform anything.

- How to utilize NLP to alter your life.

- How to quit living in the past.

Travel

Do you enjoy taking a trip? Have you been, or intend to go, on a journey all around the world? Can you offer suggestions for the best things to do in well-liked nations and cities? Do you wish to spend your life traveling the globe and taking pleasure in fresh experiences? A lot of other folks do too! It holds true that there are currently a great deal of travel vlogs out there; however, there is constantly space for more. Simply do something different from others. Here are a couple of ideas:

- Awesome locations you won't have visited.

- The expert guide to trendy tourist destinations.

- Locating those separated beaches.

- How to get by in a certain [place] - The leading 10 locations you need to go to.

- The ideal method to pack a traveling bag.

- Traveling on a budget.

Music

Are you a performer? Can you show individuals how to play an instrument or how to sing effectively? Do you understand a great deal about retro music? Music is big on YouTube and excellent "how-to" videos are constantly prominent. Here are several ideas:

- How to operate the guitar.

- How to perform with the drums.

- How to repair a damaged instrument.

- The most effective guitars (or whichever instrument).

- How to read and compose music.

- Popular track covers.

- How to compose terrific lyrics.

- The greatest bands of a category, a year etc. - How to utilize an audio editor to blend the music.

- Music tools reviews.

Pets

A few of the most prominent YouTube videos have to do with pets. Everybody has actually seen an amusing cat video or a dog carrying out unique tricks. There are lots of animal enthusiasts worldwide and they just cannot get enough material about pets. Here are several fantastic video ideas:

- How to look after your pet.

- How to instruct your dog-- numerous possibilities here.

- How to instruct your cat/dog to perform tricks.

- The ideal clothing for your cat/dog.

- The most effective names for your fresh pet.

- The ideal accessories for your pet.

- How to brush your pet.

25

- Unusual pets.

- Taking a trip with your pet.

- The most suitable meals for your pet.

Beauty

Are you somebody who understands how to use makeup properly? Are you in touch with all the most recent trends? Can you offer suggestions and recommendations for softer and cleaner skin? This marketplace is huge and the need for information is going to constantly exist. Here are several terrific video ideas:

- Various makeup tutorials.

- How to make your skin appear more youthful.

- How to look after your hair.

- The ideal clothing for the bigger individual.

- The current style accessories you need to have.

- How to select the ideal attire for the event.

- The very best shoes for ladies.

- The current style trends.

- How to appear spectacular on a budget.

Cooking, Recipes and Food

Can you show individuals how to cook? Can you demonstrate to them how to make excellent tasting dishes? Do you have excellent recipes to impart? Do you understand the very best dining establishments? Can you inform individuals what to eat when they go to particular states or cities? Food is a big topic and constantly sought after. Here are several remarkable video ideas:

- How to prepare [something] - The best meals in a certain area - The leading 10 restaurants in a certain place - How to create healthy treats.

- The ideal foods for slimming down.

- Tropical cooking.

- The essential kitchen tools.

- How to put together food effectively.

- How to bake the best cakes.

- Meals that are going to thrill your household.

- What to eat whenever you are going to a certain city.

I hope that you find these ideas motivating. Producing a vlog which contains "how-to" videos is an excellent way to go, and you are going to have the ability to generate income from it in a variety of various methods. This is not a comprehensive list whatsoever, so have a good look at what you understand and establish a strategy for your vlog.

Chapter 3: Launching a Prosperous Vlog

An effective vlog is going to need a little bit of preparation. Sure, you can simply head out there with your mobile phone and begin recording video footage about your enthusiasm. However, it is much better to spend some time to consider the kind of material that you wish to show individuals and where you are going to share it.

What is the Aim of Your Vlog?

It is an excellent idea to specify the objective of your vlog. It is not an excellent idea to put in 6 months doing so! So think of your vlog as a means for you to interact with your target market. What is the general story that you wish to depict here? Here are several examples:

- I am going to take you to travel locations, which you will not believe.

- I am going to demonstrate to you how to quickly generate income on the internet from home.

- I am going to demonstrate to you how to appear stunning each day on a budget plan.

- I am going to deliver all the current updates and fan responses for a certain sports team.

Do you understand? Excellent. You wish to make your vlog stand apart from the rest. Have a look at a number of the existing vlogs on the market which have a big subscriber base for motivation. Just do not devote too much time doing this!

Pick Your Vlogging Style

The moment you are starting with vlogging, it is ideal to perform what you are comfy with. You are going to want to reveal your face on camera-- there is no sidestepping this. Viewers are not going to be thrilled if they never ever see you in the videos. It is going to assist in driving engagement. There are various kinds of vloggers. Some are going to wish to involve their partner, their kids, their buddies, their pets etc. in their vlogs. A great deal of vloggers are going to record video footage when they are outdoors doing something. Others are going to utilize their office or home for their vlogging. Will you film all of the video footage on your own, or will another person aid you? In case you will film the video footage yourself and intend to perform this outside as you are walking around, you can utilize particular tools to accomplish this.

Are you generally funny? If so then constantly infuse some humor into your vlog. Consider other manners in which you could keep viewers amused. Making errors with vlogging is fantastic due to the fact that you can reveal the outtakes of when things failed. So think of the design you are going to utilize for your vlog. How could you make your personality actually radiate through and keep individuals involved and desiring more videos?

What are Other Vloggers Doing?

In case there is competition for your vlogging niche, go and have a look at what your rivals are doing. Spend some time to see their videos and discover what they do. Begin with the most prominent vlogs and work your way down. Here are several things to keep an eye out for:

- What are the topics of their videos?

- Which of their videos are the most well-known and for what reason?

- What is the typical duration of their videos?

- What engagement strategies do they utilize?

- Do they have sponsors or endorse affiliate items?

- How frequently do they post fresh videos?

In the event that your time is minimal, then simply study the leading vloggers in your industry. Look for these vlogs on YouTube, and after that, select those with the greatest amount of members and video views. This is going to be time extremely well spent and ought to provide you with a great deal of excellent ideas.

Determine and Understand Your Audience

What type of audience are you searching for? Will your vlog be for individuals who wish to take a trip to amazing locations throughout the world? Or find out how to earn money on the internet? Or discover how to look lovely utilizing budget plan makeup? Discover as much about your audience as you are able to. What do they truly wish to know? What are the typical concerns which they have? What blog sites or vlogs do they go to now?

What Vlog Brand Name Will You Utilize?

You require a name for your channel and vlog. You might utilize your personal name for this and plenty of individuals have actually achieved success doing this. Or you could select a particular name for your vlog, which shows what it refers to. Here are several instances. (A few of these might, in fact, exist so examine first):

- Stunning You-- a makeup vlog.
- Unique Locations - a travel vlog.

- Online Earnings-- make money on the web vlog.

So it is time for you to get a tad imaginative. Plan ahead when you are conceptualizing vlog name ideas. With an effective vlog, you could develop and promote your own products, so an appealing name is going to definitely assist here.

Why You Need To Release Your Vlog on YouTube

Here are certain engaging reasons why you need to establish your vlog on YouTube:

- There are more than 1 billion people on YouTube.

- Each day YouTube receives 4 billion video views.

- You could be successful in any YouTube niche.

- Mobile phones represent 1 billion views each day.

Is that amazing enough for you? Look, individuals like to view videos on all sorts of various topics. They are going to utilize YouTube as an online search engine to discover what they desire. It is the second biggest online search engine on the planet after Google. In case your channel offers what those searchers are trying to find, then you are going to get views. You can then inform your visitors to go and check out your site (or Facebook page etc.) for more amazing things. Provide an excellent reward to join your e-mail list, and they are going to do it. Yes, there are other video websites like Vimeo and Daily Motion. These websites get a respectable quantity of traffic; however, they are miles from YouTube. If anybody informs you that YouTube is saturated then simply disregard them. It is the only way for your vlog.

Develop Channel Art and Your YouTube Channel

A YouTube channel with no channel art does not generate an excellent impression. So invest time creating and designing suitable channel art for your vlog. In case graphic design is not your thing, then head to Fiverr.com and locate somebody who is proficient at it. Tell them what your channel is going to be about and provide your ideas for the channel art style. It is going to just cost you a couple of dollars to have fantastic channel art developed. This is well worth it. You are going to additionally require a little image for your channel symbol. This is your vlog logo.

When you have actually decided on this, you are able to include it into all of your videos and on your promoting moving forward. If you do not currently have a YouTube account, then you are going to want to make a cost-free Google account at https://www.google.com/. This is really simple to do and is going to require you less than 5 minutes. With your Google account established to go to YouTube.com and log in with your Google account. Then head to https://www.youtube.com/create_channel and make your vlog channel utilizing your brand name. After establishing your channel, I strongly advise that you develop a custom-made URL for your channel. To accomplish this, your YouTube account has to be more than one month old and you are going to require approximately 100 channel subscribers. You are going to additionally require an image of yourself and channel art. As soon as you are at this point, head to https://support.google.com/youtube/answer/2657968?hl=en for accurate directions on how to develop your custom-made channel URL. This is truly worth doing.

Plan the Content You Are Going To Develop

Okay, so your channel is good to go and the following action is to post some videos. Have a look at other effective vlogs for motivation here. How did they begin? Consider including aspects to your videos that you are going to feature constantly. For some, this is going to be a peek at the comments. For other folks, this is a recap.

If individuals enjoy these identifiable portions, they are going to return for more and are highly likely to subscribe. Plan the initial couple of weeks of video development, and after that, set up these. Dedicating these to a schedule is going to assist to inspire you. Keep in mind that consistency is the trick to a prosperous vlog.

Chapter 4: Producing Great Videos

It is simply sound judgment that you wish to develop the most appealing, inspiring and helpful videos that you can. Eventually, after a certain amount of time devoted to producing videos for your vlog, you might well discover that you can develop excellent videos on the fly. Until you reach that stage, I suggest that you follow the actions listed beneath.

Develop a Script

The majority of folks simply can't sit in front of a video camera and talk easily about their topic. In the event that you can, then terrific-- if not, then the ideal thing to do is to produce a script. Consider what you wish for every video to accomplish when preparing your script. Do you want the audience to act after viewing? The most vital parts of a video are the start and completion. Make the beginning actually engaging to inspire the audience to view all the way through. Remember that many folks have extremely short attention spans, and in case you do not make a great start with your videos, then even enthusiastic fans are not going to view the video.

You want to make the conclusion of the video really motivating too. This is specifically essential if you wish for them to take a particular action, such as checking out your site. In case you have no particular call to action in your mind, then provide a flavor of what the following video is going to be about. Make certain that your video script flows smoothly. In case you will demonstrate to your audience how to perform something then plan what you want to carry out and when. In case you are filming outdoors, then where are you going to go initially, secondly, and so on? After preparing your script, develop a storyboard. In case you are planning to narrate over the top of the video, then practice this. Keep in mind to maintain your videos as brief as you are able to. In case a tutorial will be lengthy, split it up into 2 or 3 videos.

What About Tools?

OK, I did state at the beginning of this manual that you might make a video for your vlog with simply your mobile phone. You could start in this manner; however, there are far better methods to create your videos. This all begins with a high-quality camcorder.

You do not require an expert digital camera to film your vlog videos. Whenever your vlog achieves success and you are bringing in income, then go and obtain a professional camera. Until then, simply utilize a high-quality camcorder which is going to film in HD. In case you will shoot videos inside, then you want to consider lighting. Record some test video footage to see how desirable the lighting is. Buy some lights in case you have to. It is useless investing in a top-quality video camera if the lighting is bad. You require a high-quality mic too. In case you develop videos with bad audio quality, then you are certainly not going to prosper with your vlog. For interior recording, acquire a premium USB microphone.

What about screen recording and video modifying? In case you are planning to produce tutorials, then you might wish to film your computer system screen. Desktop recording is simple with Camtasia; however, this is going to be priced at around $200. There is a cost-free alternative which is CamStudio. Give this a shot initially. CamStudio is going to just work on Windows-based computer systems. In case you have a Mac, then you can have a go at macOS Mojave. There are additional cost-free screen recording apps for Macs. After recording your video, you are going to want to edit it to render it the very best it could be. If you have Camtasia or CamStudio at that point, both of these are going to do an excellent job. There are cost-free video editing apps accessible for Mac and Windows users. Windows Movie Maker is an excellent video editing set for Windows users, and in case you own a Mac, then utilize iMovie. You are going to find both of these apps user-friendly and you can include shifts and other functions to produce your videos appear truly fantastic.

Developing Your Video

Talk with enthusiasm in your voice. Do not be dull and boring. This is going to drive individuals away quicker than you could envision. Be passionate during the video. You simply cannot expect your viewers to be passionate about your videos if you are not. If you are developing a tutorial, then offer evidence that your approaches truly work. If other individuals utilize your approaches, then ask them to supply a video review. Include as much social proof as you are able to. Appeal to individuals' feelings as much as feasible within your video. Tell them how interesting it is going to be for them to take a trip to the location you are shooting in. Or tell them how gorgeous they are going to look after utilizing your make up ideas.

Test How Well Your Videos are Received.

In your head, you have actually developed an excellent video; however, what truly counts is what your audience believes. You want to take a look at a couple of things here, like the number of viewers who saw your video from start to finish? If that wasn't the case for a great deal of viewers, at what phase of the video did they quit viewing it? Is there an issue with a particular part of the video? How many individuals liked the video, and how many provided it with a "thumbs down"?

Check out the remarks and see if there are any critiques there. Do not take them individually. Treat them as great feedback to produce greater videos down the road. What can you do in case your video was not effectively received? Well, you may either edit it to include the information that individuals in the comments state was lacking, or you can produce a brand-new video which deals with this. So now you understand how to develop excellent videos which are going to keep individuals engaged and desiring more from your vlog. Choose the majority circulation. With all videos, you can always count on people who have a grievance. In case most of the viewers love your video, then you are on the correct track.

Constantly ask viewers of your videos to sign up for your channel in case they have not. Ask them to "like" the video too and motivate them to leave comments to ensure that you could produce greater videos in the future. Inform your audience that your vlog is for them, so any feedback is really useful. Do whatever you are able to to appeal to individuals' feelings. Tell them that they can accomplish whatever you are demonstrating to them. Utilize words like "amazing," "great" and other superlatives. And constantly be enthusiastic in your videos!

Chapter 5: Optimizing Your Youtube Videos

Optimizing your videos correctly is vital. When you are first beginning, this is truly crucial as you want to do whatever that you can to guarantee that your videos show up in a YouTube search. It is going to additionally increase your odds of your videos ranking higher in Google too.

All of it Begins With Keyword Research

You want to learn what individuals are most likely to type into the search box on YouTube to discover your videos. The ideal method to accomplish this is through keyword research. You might do this completely free, utilizing the Google Keyword Planner. You will need to make a cost-free Google Adwords account to gain access to this tool. Let's state that you are developing a video about taking a trip to

Japan. When you are in the Google Keyword Planner type in the seed keyword "Japan Travel" and after that, see what other keyword recommendations Google has to provide. You can download these ideas in a CSV file which you can open with the majority of spreadsheet applications like Microsoft Excel. Look at the list and pick the ideal keywords. Take a look at the approximated search volumes. You wish to create a list of around 10 keywords for every video. Choose which keyword is going to be your "primary" keyword. Perhaps this could be "travel to Japan."

Produce a Compelling Headline Around Your Primary Keyword

You want to come up with an attractive headline so that when individuals see your video in the search results page, they will wish to see it. So for our Japan instance, you might utilize something like "Travel To Japan For Fun And Enjoyment." Make certain that you include your primary keyword in the title. Do not simply leave the title as "Travel To Japan." This will not influence that many folks to view your video. Utilize other words to produce enthusiasm. Another method might be "Travel To Japan-- You Will Not Believe What Happened!" This produces interest. Attempt composing a variety of various titles with your keyword in them. Choose 10 various titles, and after that, pick the very best one. In case you can get the keyword in at the start of the title, at that point, this is more suitable, yet it doesn't matter that much. So simply go crazy here with your ideas. Keep in mind that the more alluring you make your title, the more views you are going to get.

Compose a Keyword-Rich Description

Some individuals like to check out the description of a video before they see it, so make this engaging also. I suggest that your description is at the very least 300 words long and includes the secondary keywords that you discovered previously. Inform individuals what the video refers to, however, do not provide everything. You can constantly state something like, "you will not believe what happened by the end of this video" or "I have a huge surprise for you by the end of the video." Simply utilize tactics to hook the audience and motivate them to see all the way through. Do not go nuts with keywords in the description. In case you can't fit them in organically, do not include them.

Utilize the Appropriate Tags for Your Video

Just utilize keywords in tags that relate to your video. If your video has to do with traveling to Japan, then do not include unassociated keywords in like "how to speak Chinese." If somebody is aiming to understand Chinese and sees your video, they are going to be really unimpressed that there is very little about learning Chinese within it. So pick about 5 associated keywords (involving your primary keyword) and include these as tags. There is a 400 character limitation on tags with YouTube at the moment of composing. This does not indicate that you need to utilize every last character.

Make Sure to Articulate your Primary Keywords in the Video

This one may amaze you. The important thing is that technology has actually truly advanced over the last couple of years, and YouTube can comprehend English (and perhaps other languages), so it will detect particular essential expressions. No one understands simply how precise the YouTube system is for acknowledging spoken keywords; however, estimates propose as high as 80%. This is going to continuously improve, so it is truly worth stating your primary keyword and certain secondary keywords within your video. Make sure to prepare for this when producing your video script.

Excellent Video Optimization Does Not Take Long

If you have actually devoted a lot of time producing a storyboard and a video script as I recommended, then it appears insane not to devote a couple of minutes optimizing your videos to ensure that they have the optimum possibility of being discovered in a search. So utilize these video optimization pointers each time. Do not avoid the keyword research phase, as this is the most crucial activity. It is not going to require you long to reveal some excellent keywords. Even if you have a big following with your vlog, I would regularly advise that you optimize every video.

Chapter 6: Promoting Your Vlog

When you produce your brand-new vlog and begin to post your videos, you need to do more than simply depend on the optimization strategies we went over in the last chapter for search traffic. You want to inform the world about your fresh vlog! It is never ever an instance of "create it and they are going to come." You want to put in some constant advertising effort to offer your vlog every opportunity of establishing a big following. Certain vloggers wait up until they have a variety of videos on their vlog like 10 to 30, yet my suggestion is to begin promoting your blog site immediately after your initial video is up. If you do not have a substantial social media following, then do not allow that to stop you. Some vloggers started with social profiles of less than 50 fans and now they are doing extremely well. The crucial thing is to be consistent.

Inform Everybody That You Know

Make a list of all of your members of the family, buddies, work coworkers previous and present and any other individuals who you know. Utilize Facebook, e-mail and any other methods that you have to call them and tell them about your brand-new vlog. In case you have not talked to a few of these individuals in years, write them a pleasant e-mail and let them know that you miss them. Ask them to connect with you once again in case you wish to do that. After that, tell them that you have actually begun a brand-new vlog and that you would truly value their help. This is something which is so simple to do; however, the majority of folks do not perform it. Unless you have a great reason for not telling individuals you currently know about your vlog, then let them know! It could be a great deal of fun reaching out to individuals you have actually not contacted in a while. Ask them to get the word out to the folks who they know as well.

Utilize Reddit

In case you do not have a Reddit account, then register for one today. It is an incredibly popular network that is neglected by the majority of people. Individuals make Sub Reddits that are devoted to particular topics and specific niches. Not all of these are going to be a winner for you. Nevertheless, here are some excellent ones for fresh vloggers:

-/ r/NewTubers.

-/ r/vlog.

-/ r/vlogs.

-/ r/vlogger.

-/ r/vlogging.

As soon as you get your Reddit account, utilize it to talk about other individuals' accounts. Attempt to develop an account which fits your vlog brand. Make sure to follow the guidelines on Reddit as you can get your account closed extremely rapidly if they believe you are spamming. Have a look at what others carry out in the Sub Reddits pointed out above.

Use Facebook

You can not and should not neglect the largest social media network. Facebook is a fantastic location for publishing videos and getting individuals to share your material. Produce a Facebook Page around your vlog brand name. It is truly simple to do and there are a lot of YouTube videos to demonstrate to you how to accomplish this successfully. Include branded artwork on your Facebook page. Make it appear truly expert. Make sure to publish other helpful material on your page along with your vlog videos. End up being friends with other individuals on Facebook that remain in your niche. Search For Facebook Groups which you could sign up with that are related as well. Facebook has an excellent marketing service where you can precisely target your audience to push traffic to your Facebook Page. It is not merely about obtaining "likes" for your page. Motivate individuals to leave comments and share too.

Use Twitter

Twitter is a big social media network that it could be tough to have success with. However, it deserves the effort due to the fact that with a big Twitter following, you could truly increase subscriptions to your vlog. Once again, do not simply create tweets about your vlogs. In case this is all that you do, then individuals are going to stop reacting to your tweets. Post some other beneficial tweets and re-tweet material from various other Twitter users that relates to your vlog. Prospering with Twitter (just like with other social networks) is all about connecting with others. Follow individuals who you think have an interest in your industry and respond to the tweets that they create and retweet them. Share their material as much as you manage.

Use Instagram

A great deal of individuals avoid Instagram since it could be challenging to get a following there. However, it is truly worth persisting with it as you are able to get a great deal of YouTube views from this network. Instagram users like photos, along with videos. So take a fascinating screenshot from your vlogs and publish this asking individuals to take a look.

Something you want to understand about Instagram is that you can't link straight to your YouTube vlog from posts. They do not enable external links. So you want to establish a great bio on Instagram and link to your vlog from there. When you create a post, inform individuals that the link to your vlog remains in your bio. It is constantly an excellent idea to inform individuals precisely what you wish for them to do.

Use Quora

Quora.com is an online forum where questions are posed on almost each subject imaginable. It has a substantial user base and is typically neglected as a marketing tool for vloggers. It is likewise a fantastic location to get motivation for potential videos for your vlog. Discover concerns which have a direct connection to videos on your vlog. Compose a response, and after that, include something such as "for a more comprehensive response to this, please have a look at this video." In case your video does a truly excellent job addressing the concern, it is going to get a great deal of "upvotes," which indicates that a growing number of Quora users are going to see it.

Make Comments on Videos Published by Prominent YouTubers

While it holds true that there are a great deal of idiots who make foolish comments on a lot of YouTube videos (you are going to need to handle this on your own at some phase), there are actually a great deal of real individuals who leave comments too. Your task is to turn into one of these authentic individuals who leave practical comments. Discover other associated videos in your niche and leave a favorable comment about it. By entering into the discussion and adding value to other individuals' videos, there is a likelihood that they are going to reciprocate by clicking your username and taking a look at your channel. This is among the most convenient and most reliable methods to get more subscribers and views, so make certain that you perform this. It is really essential that you select the videos of prominent YouTubers who have some relation to your vlog. You do not need to simply include positive comments to popular videos either. Discover other associated top-quality videos which do not have as many views and add comments to those as well. Do not utilize a spam technique here-- never ever ask the video poster to take a look at your channel and subscribe.

Utilize the YTTalk Online Forum

Sign up with the YTTalk online forum. It is an extremely active online forum for the YouTube community, and there are individuals there with little and big channels. Begin adding to other individuals' posts and after that, utilize the online forum as a feedback system for your videos. Individuals who publish videos on YouTube have a tendency to view other individuals' videos too, so this is an excellent place to discover additional subscribers and viewers. As always, seek to bring in value with your posts and responses. Do not turn to any kind of spam.

Use Empire.Kred

Many vlog owners have actually never ever even heard of Empire.Kred. When you register, you are granted a stock value based upon your social impact. You can publish your vlog material here and convince other influencers on the platform to take a look and engage with it. Other influencers on Empire.Kred could acquire stock in you in case they enjoy what you are doing. This is going to boost the quantity of "eaves" that you possess (the digital currency utilized). You could utilize your eaves to develop particular tasks like asking for other influencers to see your newest video and so on. You are not permitted to request particular engagement activities like sharing, commenting or liking. Simply leave it to the influencer to generate their own choices on this. Influencers are going to gain eaves from you for finishing the job. In case the influencers enjoy your vlog, they are going to register for your channel.

Engage With All Comments You Get

The ideal method to promote your vlog is to develop a community. As you expand your community, increasingly more individuals are going to return to your videos and share them, leave comments and like them. You want to keep an eye on comments on all of your videos and react to them as quickly as you are able to. Individuals are going to actually value that you put in the time to react to their comments. You are showing that you are a genuine individual and appreciate what they have to state. This is going to inspire them to subscribe in case they have not currently done so and watch out for your potential videos.

Chapter 7: Free Tools for Growing Your Youtube Channel

There are certain necessary resources which you could utilize to expand your YouTube channel, and the bright side is that they are all free of charge. The majority of them are simple to utilize and the advantages are quite apparent. Let's have a look at a few of the most effective cost-free tools.

TubeBuddy

The significant advantage of utilizing TubeBuddy is that it is going to conserve you a great deal of time. It likewise supplies you with some excellent guidelines to truly grow your YouTube channel. TubeBuddy is an internet browser app that works with the most frequently utilized internet browsers like Mozilla Firefox, Google Chrome, and Safari. When you utilize TubeBuddy, you are going to discover that it has lots of beneficial functions from examining the SEO of your videos to assisting you with promoting your channel. There are thorough training videos offered that discuss everything truly well. You could actually conserve hours every week with this app. You could do a lot with the cost-free variation of TubeBuddy, and I recommend that you begin with this. If you desire more functions, then there is a Pro plan offered for $9 a month, a Star bundle for $19 a month, and a Legend plan for $49 a month.

YouTube Creator Studio

This is one more cost-free app that is excellent for examining the efficiency of your channel and videos on the go. You can't really handle your videos with this app; however, you could do anything else. It is fantastic for discovering simply how well your videos are doing, as well as taking a look at the general functionality of your channel no matter where you are. There is a filter function where you could react to comments and develop that necessary connection with your audience. This function alone makes the app worth setting up on your mobile phone.

Buffer.com

I described to you in the prior chapter that utilizing social networks to grow your YouTube channel and vlog is extremely advised. To assist you in sharing your videos on social media networks, the Buffer app is a truly fantastic resource. With Buffer, you could arrange and publish your material on Facebook, Instagram, Twitter, LinkedIn and Pinterest. There is one easy control panel for handling every little thing. The cost-free Buffer plan is for no more than 3 social profiles, and you can arrange 10 posts a month as a single user.

In case you possess more than 3 social profiles or plan to create more than 10 posts a month, then there are premium plans you may opt for beginning at $15 a month. Whichever plan you select, you are going to conserve a great deal of time in case you utilize Buffer to arrange your posts. There is a web browser extension which you could utilize to publish content instantly to Facebook, Pinterest and Twitter.

Audio Hero

It might be a genuine difficulty to discover terrific royalty-free music for your YouTube videos. Audio Hero makes discovering excellent music and sound effects for your videos truly simple. There is a substantial library of more than 250,000 music clips and sound effects to pick from, so you ought to never ever have any trouble discovering what you desire. Even though the Audio Hero app is free of charge, to utilize the soundtracks, you are going to need to pay a little fee. This is a lot more desirable than running the risk of encroaching on copyright and even having your videos eradicated. During the time of composing, you can acquire 50 downloads of royalty-free music clips for just $9.99.

Snappa

Developing your personal graphics or discovering a great and dependable graphic designer might be a genuine headache. You understand that you require top quality graphics to expand your YouTube channel, so what do you do? Simply utilize Snappa, obviously! There are a great deal of premade design templates you can utilize in Snappa. You could utilize Snappa quickly to produce your preliminary channel art for truly appealing video thumbnails as you publish your videos. It is actually crucial that your thumbnails look terrific. This could actually be the distinction between someone viewing your video and another person's. The cost-free variation has 5,000 design templates and you are able to develop 5 graphics a month. In case you desire more, then plans begin at $10 a month.

Repost for Instagram

Repost for Instagram is one more beneficial app for your Android or iPhone phone. You really should take Instagram into consideration as an excellent social platform to promote your vlog. It has a big user base which is growing constantly. When you have the Repost for Instagram app, you are going to have the ability to repost images or videos that your fans shared. You could incorporate the username of the individual that shared the material so that they get the credit, and your fans can quickly check them out.

Chapter 8: Methods to Monetize Your Vlog

OKAY, so you have your YouTube channel established properly, you have actually published some vlog videos and you are striving to boost your subscriber amount and video views. Where is the benefit in all of this? This manual has to do with vlogging for income, so I will show you a few of the very best methods to generate income from your vlog here. The reality is that there are various manners in which you could generate income from your videos and vlog.

YouTube Partner

When you end up being a YouTube Partner, you are able to show Google Adsense advertisements on videos that you pick. If you are not familiar with Google Adsense, it is utilized by publishers

74

(like vloggers and blog site owners) to show Google Advertisements in or on their content. Each time an advertisement is clicked you share the income with YouTube. Now the initial thing to state here is that it is not likely that you are going to make life-altering earnings with Google Adsense on your videos even if you have countless views. There are likewise numerous aspects which impact just how much of the income you get like:

- The amount of views an advertisement gets (not all viewers of your video are going to discover the advertisement).

- The duration of time that the advertisement was visible (some advertisements are really brief videos).

- Was there any engagement with the advertisement?

- The demographics of your target market.

- The number of marketers that wish to promote in your niche at the existing time.

As you have actually most likely figured out, it is hard to forecast the cash you are going to make by making it possible for Google Adsense on your videos. However, you do not need to stress over any of the aspects above, aside from attempting to get as many views to your video as achievable. There are various kinds of Google Adsense advertisements that you can show on your videos. Among the most typical is a basic banner showing at the base of the video. There are likewise brief video trailers which could be shown at the beginning, throughout your video or at the conclusion. In some cases, the audience is able to skip these trailers and on other occasions, they are going to need to view them.

You are going to have to fulfill a variety of requirements to be qualified for the YouTube Partner Program and showing Google Adsense advertisements. The guidelines alter typically, so it is ideal to go to https://support.google.com/youtube/answer/72851#eligibility to see what the most recent guidelines are. As soon as you are a verified partner, it is simple to generate income from any of your videos by logging into your YouTube profile and making it possible for monetization. There are a variety of payment approaches which you could select from consisting of a check, electronic funds transfer, wire transfer, Western Union and more. You want to think thoroughly about making it possible for these advertisements on your videos. Some audiences are not going to mind an Adsense banner at the base of the video. A trailer at the beginning which can not be skipped might try out the patience of several visitors though, particularly in case they are brand-new to your vlog.

Affiliate Marketing

With affiliate marketing, you advertise other individuals' items and when a sale is made, you make a commission. Commissions vary from extremely little (a couple of cents) to huge (hundreds of dollars) for high ticket products. Videos are a great deal more convincing than composed text, so you might be showing an item or a piece of software application while including your affiliate link within the description. Certain individuals who own makeup vlogs for instance succeed on a monthly basis via affiliate marketing. With a lot of vlog specific niches, there are going to be affiliate services and products which you could advertise. You simply want to discover them. Utilize Google or another online search engine and enter the kind of service or a product, and after that, "affiliate program." So an instance would be "cosmetics affiliate program." You can advertise physical items and digital items too. Digital items would generally be software applications, a "how-to" guide, instruction videos, and so forth. It could be more difficult to make a sale with digital items, yet the commissions are typically a great deal higher than with tangible goods.

Merchandising

You could develop your personal merchandising for your vlog brand. A fine instance of this is a t-shirt or sweatshirt with your brand name logo on it or perhaps caps. There are businesses you could utilize that are going to provide the clothing or caps in the appropriate sizes and colors with your design engraved on them. There are other merchandising items which are rather simpler than clothing like USB memory sticks with your logo design, calendars with your logo, pens with your logo design, phone cases, and a lot more. It is simple to discover a business which is going to brand prominent products for you. Merchandising is not a thing which you have to consider when you are initially beginning with your vlog. You are going to require a great deal of active subscribers to earn a profit from merchandising. Once you attain that big subscriber foundation, then you can offer a great deal of merchandise products and bring in good cash.

Offering Your Own Products/Services

This is something which you may do relatively rapidly with your vlog. There are various services and products that you are able to offer from your vlog. Here are certain instances:

- A book.

- A "how-to" tutorial.

- A video training course.

- Training services.

The ideal method to accomplish this is to instruct your audience about the essentials of accomplishing something, and after that, inform them that they require your product in case they would like to know the advanced techniques. Offer value within your videos to get your audience hooked, however, do not deliver everything free of charge. Among the most ideal methods to offer your services and products is via e-mail marketing. You could utilize an e-mail autoresponder service like Aweber or get a response and offer something of value free of charge as a reward for joining your e-mail list. You are going to want to do this from your site or blog site and after that include this link in your video description. Inform individuals in your videos of the advantages of joining your e-mail list. Tell them that you are going to supply them with more cost-free ideas and recommendations, but just if they register for your list.

Brand Sponsorship

In case you can get a brand name sponsorship offer, then you do not need to stress over showing advertisements or offering anything. You are going to get payment from the sponsor due to the fact that they want you to advertise what they provide on your vlog. It is immediately related to your vlog and is going to assist your audience. You are going to want to touch on your sponsor in the videos. The majority of the time, sponsors discover vloggers. They will just wish to deal with vloggers who have a big subscriber base, so this could require some time to occur. In case you have a great deal of subscribers and your videos have big view counts, at that point, the sponsors are going to call you.

Financing Platforms

There are now funding platforms like Patreon.com which make it possible for vlog fans to establish a month to month membership to finance their preferred vloggers and keep them going. A great deal of vloggers are now relying on platforms such as Patreon for a routine month-to-month earnings. With Patreon, you can set different levels of memberships. You are going to want to provide your Patreon subscribers with something more than what your regular vlog subscribers get. They want to feel unique and pleased that they are financing you monthly.

Chapter 9: Vlogging Best Practices

In case you want your vlog to be effective, there are a couple of best practices that I strongly suggest that you embrace. These best practices are followed by all effective vloggers, so you want to pay very close attention here and comply with them too.

Constantly Produce Top Quality Videos

Constantly put your audience first. What are they searching for? Which responses do they require to resolve issues in their life? How can you make their life more interesting and how could you captivate your audience? Never ever submit low-grade videos to your vlog since you feel under pressure to provide your audience with something. It is constantly about quality and not quantity. If you produce something of poor quality, then you are going to lose your audience. Simply do not do this! Utilize excellent tools and software applications to develop your videos. You do not need the most pricey digital camera on the marketplace, however, you do have to produce videos which are clear with great sound quality. Never ever utilize a poor-quality mic. Constantly be enthusiastic and delighted in your videos. In case you are not enthusiastic, how could you expect your viewers to be?

Consistency

When you begin pumping out your top quality videos, then your audience is going to yearn for increasingly more from you. You want to be consistent and produce videos to a schedule of some type. If you leave it too long between one video and the following, you are going to lose individuals. You want to be persistent with your vlog. OK, several vlogs have actually taken off truly rapidly and made their owners a great deal of cash in record time.

However, this is the exception instead of the rule. Take your time and be persistent and concentrate on being dependable with quality and publishing schedules.

Concentrate on Getting More Subscribers

Do not concentrate on cash; concentrate on getting brand-new subscribers. Do whatever you are able to to get the word out about your vlog. When the subscribers arrive, so will the cash. Utilize social networks thoroughly and attempt other approaches to promote your vlog.

Know What is Working

YouTube has a great deal of analytics to assist you in figuring out what your videos are doing the best. So, utilize this to find what is working and what is not. Do more of what is working! Fine-tune things to make them much better. Examine your videos for the right optimization approach.

Chapter 10: Installing the Game

The game that we will be playing and recording is called DOTA 2. You can choose other games but this is the one I recommend you get started with.

To install this, you need to get STEAM first. This serves as the mother server for all the famous online games today.

Once installed, create your own free account.

Then search for DOTA 2 and download the game. It's free.

It's quite a big file so be patient and just do something else while you're waiting for it to finished.

Once you complete your download, Go to library tab on Steam and click on PLAY.

Then open the Settings by clicking the gear button on the upper left of the screen. Then open the VIDEO tab.

Next to the DISPLAY button, click the dropdown and choose borderless window.

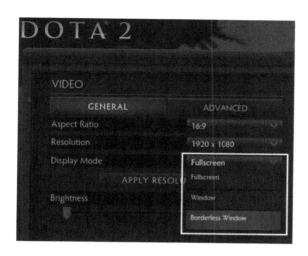

You're finished for now.

How to Start Your Youtube Channel

We have to create a youtube channel specifically for DOTA 2.

Click the link below to get a good example.

For starters, there's only 3 important factor to consider for your channel (besides the videos itself).

The first one is the CHANNEL NAME

Make sure that you choose a name that relates to DOTA.

Ex.

DotaGamers2

DotaAddict

DOTA2Magicians

The second factor to consider is your cover image.

This is so important that I recommend that you don't do this yourself unless you know how to edit images.

You viewers will see this when they visit your profile and your cover image can help a lot in getting someone to subscribe to your account.

Hire someone on Fiverr to do it for you.

It's only $5 and you'll get a better cover compared to you doing it yourself.

The third one is your Profile Picture. For this one, I suggest that you find some

DOTA characters in Google Images and choose one.

Recording Your or Other People's Games

We don't need to record the whole game, some people do watch whole games but I'd rather focus on creating 3 videos a day with 5 minutes length each than a one 1 hour video.

First, launch camtasia and then DOTA 2.

Click WATCH

You will then see a list of premium, professional and amateur tournaments.

We'll just focus on premium and professional since those are where the game worth watching and recording happens.

Some of the premium games will cost you $10, normally you could see some 80-100 games on that $10 premium.

Not all people will bother paying these fees, if you want an advantage and less competition, buy the premium games and record them all.

What Games to Choose:

I normally record anything under premium and professional. Just don't bother with amateur and you are set.

To choose a game, click the dropdown arrow.

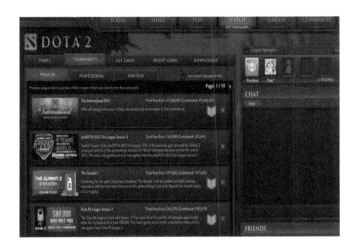

You will see something like this one below.

Click another dropdown and choose a game.

Click the download button.

After downloading (2-10 minutes)

Click Watch Highlights.

And then open your recorder, then CLICK
record on your camtasia. Or you can press
F9 instead of manually clicking record.

Wait for the highlights to finished and
then stop recording. Press F10 for the
STOP recording shortcut.

To Summarize

1 - Select a game/tournament

2- Download the replay

3- Watch Highlights

4- Record from start to finish

5 - Save and Edit

Chapter 11: One Minute Video Editing

I fucking hate editing videos.

That's why I don't do it!

Here's what to do after finishing the recordings.

Save the file on a new folder.

Once Camtasia launches, a window will pop up, asking you to edit the dimensions. Select "1280x720" and click on "OK."

Cut the part where the game still haven't started and the part where you're still recording even though the game is already finished. And you're done. Yup.

Open the "File" menu and select "Produce and Share."

Select "MP4 only (up to 720p)." Name your video and save it to your hard drive.

Uploading Your Video

When you upload your video, there are some things that you need to remember to maximize the "search power" of your video.

Here are the things you need to implement to make sure that you'll have a o lot of views online.

Title

Your title should have the exact keyword phrase you are targeting. Plus add some exciting keywords like...

CRAZY GAME - AntiViceral Vs. Squadron13 - DOTA 2 Finals Tournament

AMAZING ENDING - TeamBoyGirls Vs. AsorcbicPoison - DOTA 2 Semi Finals

Short Video is Better

Try to make your videos as short as possible. Five to 10 minutes is a perfect start.

The File name

Make sure that you file name has your main keyword in it.

Example:

DOTA2NATUSVINCEREvsVEGASQUADRON. mov

The Google algorithm loves it when a file name is related to your video content because it let Google know that the video is about that topic.

Title Stacking

Putting your keyword twice in the title will help your google rankings.

Make sure though that your title makes sense and you're not just spamming the crap out of youtube.

Ex.

DOTA 2 Natus Vincere vs. Vega Squadron - Best Fight Ever - Best Vega Squadron Comeback Fight - June 2015

It repeats your keyword *Vega Squadron* but with variation.

The Channel Name

Your channel name should be related to your keyword as much as possible.

Ex. Main keyword is "DOTA 2 Natus Vincere vs. Vega Squadron"

Your channel name could be –

DOTA2highlightreels

Dota2bestgames

Dota2internationalgames

Just pick something that has some of your keywords in it.

Video Description

One of the most important parts of your video is your description. It has three purposes.

First, it let the viewers know what it is they are watching.

Second, you can use it to link out to your website or to any website where you want your viewers to go

Third, it helps Google in determining what the content is about. It also helps in rankings since it is part of Youtube-Google algorithm.

You must put http:// on your url to make it clickable.

Today, I recommend that you put a 250 words description on your video. Tell them what they can expect in the video, what games will they see etc

G. Annotation

It is good practice to put at least one or two annotations related to your topic. Don't spam your video with annotations, your viewers might get irritated and leave your page.

IMPORTANT NOTE:

DON'T MISS THIS - THIS IS HOW YOU WILL MAKE MONEY!

Make sure that you enable monetization for your video in the CHANNEL SETTING part then click "Monetization" tab.

Upper right side of your Youtube tab. Click your profile picture and settings.

If you can't find it, you can just go here while you're still login to your account.

https://www.youtube.com/account_monetization

Monetization

Account Status

Your account is not enabled for monetization. Enabling your account allows you to monetize your videos.

Having at least one video approved for monetization makes you a YouTube partner, which provides you with opportunities to improve. Learn more about the benefits of becoming a YouTube partner.

Enable My Account

Guidelines and Information

▸ How can my videos make money?
▸ How much will my videos earn?
▾ What types of videos are eligible?

For a video to be eligible, you must own worldwide commercial usage rights to everything in the video and the video must abide by Guidelines.

This means you have created everything in your video yourself, and you did not sell exclusive commercial usage rights to someone created by someone else, you must have their written permission to use and make money from it.

You may also share in the monetization of eligible cover videos. Learn more

Click ENABLE MY ACCOUNT.

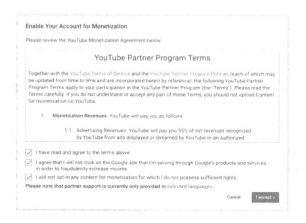

Enable Your Account for Monetization

Please review the YouTube Monetization Agreement below

YouTube Partner Program Terms

Together with the YouTube Terms of Service and the YouTube Partner Program Policies (each of which may be updated from time to time and are incorporated herein by reference), the following YouTube Partner Program Terms apply to your participation in the YouTube Partner Program (the "Terms"). Please read the Terms carefully. If you do not understand or accept any part of these Terms, you should not upload Content for monetization on YouTube.

1. **Monetization Revenues.** YouTube will pay you as follows:

    1.1   Advertising Revenues. YouTube will pay you 55% of net revenues recognized by YouTube from ads displayed or streamed by YouTube or an authorized

☑ I have read and agree to the terms above.

☑ I agree that I will not click on the Google ads that I'm serving through Google's products and services in order to fraudulently increase income.

☑ I will not opt-in any content for monetization for which I do not possess sufficient rights.

Please note that partner support is currently only provided in selected languages.

Cancel   I accept's

Step 6 - Promote Your Video

The easiest way I know to promote your video is via Facebook. Join Facebook groups about DOTA and then post your replays.

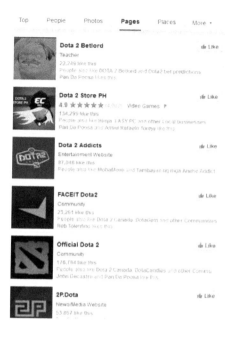

I swear by this method, You can easily join dota 2 groups on Facebook and update them with new videos every day. Many people will be glad to see replay of their favorite teams on youtube.

Also, it's also a good way to know what videos they want to see. If they want a certain team, then record that team. It's like you're getting live feedback from your audience, then you just give them what they want. In the end, you'll get more views (more adsense income) and happy viewers.

Expand

For this part, you just have to follow the system over and over again. You just need to find more games to play or record.

I recommend that you create a minimum of 3 videos a day. It shouldn't take you 2 hours to finish the process from start to finish.

Some other profitable games where you could do the same:

League of Legends

http:// leagueoflegends.com/

Minecraft

https://minecraft.net/

Smite

http://www.smitegame.com/

World of Warcraft

http://us.battle.net/wow/en/

NBA GAMES

Step 8 - How to Monetize Your Content

This step is for people who are outside Western countries- which means they are not allowed to directly monetize their video via the youtube monetization settings.

Video Monetization

Go to your channel's homepage and click on the "Edit" pencil icon that is at the bottom-right of your channel's cover photo. From the menu that pops up, select "Channel settings."

There, change your channel's country to a Western country (U.S., France, Germany, United Kingdom, etc…) then save settings.

You should now be able to enable the monetization part of your Video Manager.

The dollar sign means it's available for monetization.

Again, to enable monetization,

In your account's settings, go to the monetization tab.

Click **Enable My Account**. You'll only see this option if your account is in good standing and hasn't been disabled for monetization.

Follow the on-screen steps to accept the YouTube monetization agreement.

Youtube Adsense

Note: Do not sign up for youtube adsense unless you already have videos uploaded. Make sure that your channel looks clean and your videos should be getting views already.

If you got that part right, then you won't have any problem signing up on youtube adsense.

Sign up here:

https://support.google.com/adsense/answer/2530958?hl=en

IMPORTANT: (Your YOUTUBE email should also be the one you would use for your YOUTUBE adsense)

Chapter 12: what is vlogging

A video blog (vlog) or "vlogging" is the setting up of a specific channel on a video sharing site such as YouTube and uploading videos on a regular basis. The goal of your vlog is to provide engaging content in a specific niche that will create a reaction from viewers and grow your following or subscriber base. Vlogging took off around ten years ago when video sharing sites such as YouTube became really popular. Videos are a lot more interesting than text based content. Most people would sooner watch a short video than read hundreds of words of text.

Can vlogging really make you money? Yes it certainly can, but you need to go about it in the right way which is what this guide is all about. We will show you how to choose a niche to vlog about, the best video platform to use, how to set up your channel correctly and a lot more.

Why should you start a Vlog?

There are many good reasons why you should start a vlog right now. The first of these is that video has tremendous impact these days. YouTube and Facebook currently dominate the world of Internet video. There is a reason that both of these platforms introduced live streaming video – it is what people want! People like to watch videos and in particular they like vlogs. Some of the most successful channels on YouTube are vlogs. Once you start to get a following for your vlog the word will spread quickly and you will get a lot more subscribers.

Vlogging is one of the best ways for you to share your talents, ideas and thoughts about a subject. When you create a vlog your audience is not expecting Hollywood movie quality – in fact quite the opposite. A vlog needs to be natural and casual and really connect with the viewer.

There are all kinds of successful vlogs out there. A lot of travel vlogs allow the vloggers to travel around the world through donations, sponsorship, affiliate

marketing and other revenue opportunities. Take a look at the popularity of reality TV – people like to watch other ordinary people doing things that they love.
 If you have a specific talent then you can show the world how you put this to good use. Once you start to build a following then there will be opportunities for you to market your skills. By demonstrating that you are really good at something in your vlog you are bound to get requests from people interested in hiring you.

Some people start a vlog because they want to document their life and create a memory to share with future generations. They have no financial aspirations for doing this. This is a guide about making money from vlogging so we wouldn't recommend this approach. However a number of vloggers who started off in this way have made passive income.

There are already some very successful vloggers on YouTube that make a significant income from their vlog. People like Roman Attwood, Lilly Singh, Casey Neistat, Zoella and Alfie Deyes are all good examples.

These people all have deals with brands where they make a significant income. Brands constantly scour YouTube for new vloggers and if they find good ones they will approach them directly with deals or sponsorship. There are so many opportunities to make money with vlogging.

You can start vlogging right now. There is no need for you to purchase expensive camera equipment to start with. If you have a smartphone which can record high quality video then you are good to go. However if you can invest in good recording equipment we would always recommend this.

When you have finished shooting your footage you can then upload this to your computer and use free video editing programs such as Windows Movie Maker for Windows machines or iMovie for Mac. Yes there are better video editors out there, but you don't need them to get started.

You don't even need a website. Use YouTube as your vlogging platform. It is a good idea to have social accounts such as Facebook, Instagram and Twitter and build a following on these so that you can let everyone know when you have launched a new video.

A number of vloggers use affiliate marketing to generate revenue. For example there are a number of successful make up and cosmetics vlogs and the owners promote products and make commissions as an affiliate.

What should your Vlog be about?

The number one rule with creating a vlog is to make it about something that you are really interested in. There are no hard and fast rules here – you can literally create a vlog about anything. But we would suggest that you follow the steps below to identify a really good vlogging subject:

1. Write a list of the things that really interest you in life. Include everything here such as things that you enjoy doing at work, in your leisure time, with your friends and so on.

2. Write a second list of the talents that you have. Don't even think that you have no talents – you will be good at some things for sure.

3. Look at these lists and think about the commercial opportunities with each interest and talent. If you are a sports fan for example and follow a particular team then is there an opportunity there for you? Some sports vlog owners are millionaires!

4. Use the Google Keyword Planner to check to see how many searches a month exist for your interests and talents. You can also search on YouTube to see what videos appear and how many views and subscribers they have.

5. Choose your vlogging subject based on the best mix of interest or talent and commercial opportunity. Most vlogging guides will tell you to just vlog about

something that you are passionate about. You will certainly need to be passionate about your vlogging, but not all subjects have the same money making potential.

6. Once you have chosen a vlogging subject or niche you will need to test to see if you can create many videos with it. People will want you to vlog often – you can't just upload one video and expect miracles. So is there enough material for you to create a weekly or monthly vlog? In the next chapter you will find some great ideas for starting a profitable vlog.

The Advantages of starting a Vlog

There are a number of advantages of a vlog over a standard blog. The main reason that people prefer to create standard blogs is that it is easier than creating a vlog. You can write a post for a standard blog fairly quickly or outsource it to a professional writer. But it is a fact that people prefer video.

With a standard blog it is very difficult to develop a following. Ranking blogs in the search engines is really tough these days, and there are people promoting different blogs all over social media. The competition is tough. Yes there is competition in vlogging, but it is a lot less intense.

• *People Vlog for more exposure* – it is easier to get visitors to a vlog than it is to a standard   blog.

• *Videos are more likely to go Viral* – you have a lot more chance of one of your vlog videos going viral than a standard blog post.

• *Videos are more interactive* – it is easier to persuade people to do something with a video than it is with a written blog post. You will be much more likely to achieve higher conversion rates with good videos.

• *Video Tutorials are really effective* – people like to know how to do certain things. If you can show them how to achieve something with a video tutorial then this is far more interesting than them having to read a long blog post with screenshots.

• *You can Vlog Live* – with the live

streaming capabilities of YouTube and Facebook you can create some videos live. If you have an important announcement to make then tell people that there will be a live stream on a certain day and at a certain time. People really like live streaming video!

- *There are a number of revenue generating opportunities* – from the YouTube Partnership Program to sponsorship, special deals with brands and affiliate marketing to name but a few, popular vlogs have many options when it comes to making money.

You need to be really committed to your vlog. If you spend a few months adding videos to your channel and then stop for a while people will easily forget you. This means that you will have wasted time and effort for nothing. If you choose a subject for vlogging and there are other vloggers on YouTube in the same niche then don't let this put you off. Remember that you are the subject of your vlog. You are different to those other vloggers with your unique personality.

Chapter 13: ideas for profitable vlogs

Sometimes it can be tough to come up with that winning idea for a vlog that will make you a healthy profit. So to help you we have some great ideas for you in this chapter. We hope that you find an idea here that you can run with.

Video Games

Are you someone that enjoys playing video games a lot? There are so many people that play video games these days and there is always room for another great vlog on the subject. New games appear all of the time, and with the rise in popularity of Amazon's Twitch.tv there is so much scope for you to create quality videos. The secret to a successful video game vlog is providing the gaming community with what they want. If they enjoy the videos you create then they will spread the word for you and your vlog will grow exponentially. Here are some ideas for videos you can create:

- You playing a specific game and cracking a level or beating a boss monster etc
- A live stream about a particular game
- A review of a game (old or new)
- Your top 10 video games
- Create a game walkthrough
- Provide gaming news videos

Tutorials or How To Videos

A lot of people search YouTube to find out how to do something. So do you have a particular set of skills or are you an expert in a particular subject? If so then a series of "how to" videos would be a great vlogging idea for you. People are always using the Internet to ask questions, and videos are far and away the most popular medium that people choose to get the answers that they need. There are just endless opportunities for "how to" video tutorials. You can definitely promote affiliate products or sell your own products on the back of a vlog like this. Here are some ideas for you:

- How to build something
- How to make money online
- Life skills
- Personal development skills
- How to get a girlfriend / boyfriend and subsequent relationship advice
- Learn a new language
- How to get that new job and keep it
- How to make money in stocks, foreign exchange etc

Computers and Tech

Do you like computers and tech gadgets? Are you an expert on mobile devices? There are so many people that just love computers and tech and would be delighted to find out what is coming next etc. The world of technology changes all of the time so you will never run out of ideas for videos. Here are some good ideas:

- Useful apps for your smartphone
- The best laptops
- How to use popular software such as Microsoft Office
- New technology reviews
- Tech product comparisons

- Computer hacks and little known shortcuts
- Create your own website
- Registering a domain name
- How to make your computer faster
- How to fix common computer problems

Weight Loss and Fitness

Do you have knowledge about how to lose weight and keep it off? Are you a fitness expert? The demand for "how to" videos in this area is huge. And the subject is so vast that you should never run out of new ideas for videos. Here are some ideas to think about:

- Weight loss tips
- Compare popular diets e.g. Paleo, Keto etc
- Healthy eating recipes
- How to avoid food and beverages that will make you gain weight
- Exercising for beginners
- How to do an exercise properly e.g. push ups
- How to get fit and ripped without going to the gym

- The benefits of yoga
- Specific yoga exercises

Personal Development

This is another huge subject. People always want to improve their lives and if you have the knowledge to help them to do this then it can open all kinds of doors for you. Here are some great ideas for videos:

- X ways to be more confident
- How to overcome your fears
- How to break through your comfort zone
- How to set goals and achieve them
- How to increase your self esteem
- How to be a great conversationalist
- How to persuade people to do anything
- How to use NLP to change your life
- How to stop living in the past

Travel

Do you like traveling? Have you been, or plan to go, on an adventure across the world? Can you provide recommendations for the best things to do in popular countries and cities? Do you want to spend your life traveling the world and enjoying new experiences? So many other people do as well! It is true that there are already a lot of travel vlogs out there but there is always room for more. Just do something different to the rest. Here are some ideas for you:

• Cool places you won't have visited
• The insider guide to a popular tourist attraction
• Finding those isolated beaches
• How to survive in [location]
• The top 10 places you must visit
• The best way to pack a suitcase
• Travelling on a budget

Music

Are you a musician? Can you teach people how to play an instrument or how to sing properly? Do you know a lot about retro music? Music is huge on YouTube and good "how to" videos are always popular. Here are some ideas for you:

- How to play the guitar
- How to play the drums
- How to sing
- How to fix a broken instrument
- The best guitars (or whatever instrument) available
- How to read and write music
- Famous song covers
- How to write great lyrics
- The best bands of [genre, decade etc]
- How to use an audio editor to mix music
- Music equipment reviews

Pets

Some of the most popular videos on YouTube are about pets. Everyone has seen a funny cat video or a dog doing special tricks. There are many animal lovers in the world and they can't get enough content about pets. Here are some great video ideas:

- How to take care of your pet (cat, dog, guinea pig, horse etc)
- How to train your dog – so many possibilities here
- How to teach your cat/dog to do tricks

- The best clothes for your cat/dog
- The best names for your new pet
- The best accessories for your new pet
- How to groom your pet
- Exotic pets
- Traveling with your pet
- The best food for your pet

Beauty

Are you someone that knows how to apply makeup correctly? Are you in touch with all the latest fashions? Can you provide tips and advice for smoother and healthier skin? This market is massive and the demand for information will always be there. Here are some great video ideas:

- Different makeup tutorials
- How to make your skin look younger
- How to take care of your hair
- The best outfits for the larger person
- The latest fashion accessories you must have
- How to chose the perfect outfit for the occasion
- The best shoes for women
- The latest fashion trends

- How to look stunning on a budget
- Manicure and pedicure tutorials

Cooking, Recipes and Food

Can you teach people how to cook? Can you show them how to create great tasting meals? Do you have great recipes to share? Do you know the best restaurants? Can you tell people what to eat when they visit specific countries or cities? Food is a huge subject and always in demand. Here are some awesome video ideas for you:

- How to cook [whatever it is]
- Eating well on a budget
- The best dishes in [location]
- The top 10 restaurants in [location]
- How to make healthy snacks
- The best foods for losing weight
- Exotic cooking
- Recipes for dishes you have never heard of
- The must have kitchen accessories
- How to prepare food properly
- How to bake perfect cakes
- Meals that will delight your family

• What to eat when you are visiting [location]

We hope that you find these ideas inspiring. Creating a vlog that contains "how to" videos is a great way to go and you will be able to monetize in a number of different ways. This is not an exhaustive list by any means, so have a good look at what you know and develop a plan for your vlog.

Chapter 14: starting successful vlog

A successful vlog will require a bit of planning. Sure you can just go out there with your smartphone and start recording footage about your passion. But it is better to take some time to think about the type of content that you want to share with people and where you will share it.

What is the Purpose of your Vlog?

It is a good idea to define the purpose of your vlog. It is not a good idea to spend 6 months doing this! So think about your vlog as a way for you to communicate with your target audience. What is the overall message that you want to portray here? Here are some examples:

• I will take you to travel destinations that you won't believe
• I will show you how to easily make money online from home
• I will show you how to look beautiful every day on a budget
• I will bring you all the latest news and fan reaction for [Sports Team]

Do you get the idea? Good. You want to make your vlog stand out from the rest. Take a look at some of the existing vlogs out there that have a large subscriber base for inspiration. Just don't spend too long on this!

Decide on your Vlogging Style

When you are starting out with vlogging it is best to do what you are comfortable with. You will need to show your face on camera — there is no getting around this. Viewers will not be impressed that they never see you in the videos. It will help to drive   engagement.
There are different types of vloggers. Some will want to include their partner, their children, their friends, their pets etc in their vlogs. A lot of vloggers will shoot footage when they are outside doing something. Others will use their home or office   for   their   vlogging.
Are you going to shoot all of the footage yourself or will someone else help you? If you are going to shoot the footage yourself and want to do this outside while

you are walking around then you can use specific tools to do this. Are you naturally funny? If so then always inject as much humor as you can into your vlog. Think about other ways that you can keep viewers entertained. Making mistakes with vlogging is great because you can show the outtakes of when things went wrong. So think about the style you will use for your vlog. How can you make your personality really shine through and keep people engaged and wanting more videos from you?

What are other Vloggers doing?

If there is competition for your vlogging niche then go and check out what your competitors are doing. Take some time out to watch their videos and see what they do. Start with the most popular vlogs and work your way down. Here are some things to look out for:

• What are the subjects of their videos?
• Which of their videos are the most popular and why?

- What is the average length of their videos?
- What engagement techniques do they use?
- Do they have sponsors or recommend affiliate products?
- How often do they upload new videos?
- What does their channel look like?
- What effects do they use in their videos if any?

If your time is limited then just study the top vloggers in your niche. Search for these vlogs in YouTube and then choose those with the highest number of subscribers and video views. This will be time very well spent and should give you lots of good ideas.

Identify and Know your Audience

What kind of audience are you looking for? Is your vlog going to be for people that want to travel to exciting destinations across the world? Or learn how to make money online? Or learn how to look beautiful using budget makeup? Find out as much about your audience as you can. What do they really want to know? What are the common questions that they have? What blogs or vlogs do they visit now? What age range are they?

What Vlog Brand will you use?

You need a name for your vlog and channel. You could use your own name for this and many people have been successful doing this. Or you can choose a specific name for your vlog which reflects what it's about. Here are some examples that we came up with (some of these may actually exist so check first):

- ***Beautiful You*** – a makeup vlog
- ***Exotic Destinations*** - a travel vlog
- ***[Sports Team] Fanzone*** – a sports team vlog
- ***Online Income*** – a make money online vlog
- ***All About Dogs*** – a dog vlog

So it is time for you to get a little creative. Think ahead when you are brainstorming vlog name ideas. With a successful vlog you can create and sell your own merchandise so a catchy name will certainly help here.

Why you must launch your Vlog on YouTube

Here are some compelling reasons why you should set up your vlog on YouTube:
• There are more than 1 billion users on YouTube
• Every day YouTube gets 4 billion video views (yes 4 billion!)
• You can succeed in any niche on YouTube
• Mobile devices account for 1 billion views per day

Is that exciting enough for you? Look people love to watch videos on all kinds of different subjects. They will use YouTube as a search engine to find what they want. It is the second largest search engine in the world after Google. If your channel provides what those searchers are looking for then you will get views. You can then tell your viewers to go and visit your website (or Facebook page etc) for more cool stuff. Give them a good incentive to join your email list and they will do it.

Yes there are other video sites such as Daily Motion and Vimeo. These sites get a pretty good amount of traffic but they are miles away from YouTube. If anyone tells you that YouTube is saturated then just ignore them. It is the only way to go for your vlog!

Create Channel Art and your YouTube Channel

A YouTube channel without channel art does not create a good impression. So spend time designing and creating appropriate channel art for your vlog. If graphic design is not your thing then go to Fiverr.com and find someone that is good at it. Tell them what your channel will be about and give them your ideas for the channel art design.

It will only cost you a few bucks to have great looking channel art created. This is well worth it. You will also need a small image for your channel icon. This is the logo for your vlog. Once you have settled

144

on this you can add it into all of your videos and on your merchandising going forward. If you don't already have a YouTube account then you will need to create a free Google account at https://www.google.com/. This is very easy to do and will take you less than 5 minutes. With your Google account set up head over to YouTube.com and log in with your Google account. Then go to https://www.youtube.com/create_channel and create your vlog channel using your brand name.

After setting up your channel we highly recommend that you create a custom URL for your channel. To do this your YouTube account needs to be more than 30 days old and you will need at least 100 channel subscribers. You will also need a photo of yourself and channel art loaded. Once you are at this point go to https://support.google.com/youtube/answer/2657968?hl=en for precise instructions on how to create your custom channel URL. This is really worth doing.

Plan the Content you will create

OK so your channel is all setup to go and the next step is to upload some videos. Take a look at other successful vlogs for inspiration here. How did they start? Think about adding elements to your videos that you will include all of the time. For some this will be a look at the comments. For others this is a recap. If people like these recognizable segments they will come back for more and are very likely to subscribe. Plan out the first few weeks of video creation and then schedule these. Committing these to a schedule will help to motivate you. Remember that consistency is the secret to a successful vlog.

Chapter 15: creating great vdeos

It is just common sense that you want to create the most engaging, inspirational and informative videos that you can. After a while of creating videos for your vlog you may well find that you can create great videos on the fly. Until you get to that stage we recommend that you follow the steps below.

Create a Script

Most people just can't sit in front of a camera and talk freely about their subject. If you can then great – if not then the best thing to do is to create a script. Think about what you want each video to achieve when planning your script. Do you want the viewer to take action after watching?

The most important parts of a video are the beginning and the end. Make the start really compelling to motivate the viewer to watch all the way through. Keep in mind that most people have very short attention spans and if you don't make a good start with your videos then even

passionate followers will not watch. You need to make the end of the video very inspiring too. This is especially important if you want them to take a specific action like visit your website. If you have no specific call to action in mind then give them a taste of what the next video will be about.
Ensure that your video script flows nicely. If you are going to show your audience how to do something then plan out what you need to do and when. If you are recording outside then where will you go first, second and so on?
After planning your script then create a storyboard. If you are going to narrate over the top of the video then practice this. Remember to keep your videos as short as you can. If a tutorial is going to be long then break it up into 2 or 3 videos.

What about Equipment?

OK we did say at the start of this guide that you could make a video for your vlog with just your smartphone. You can get started this way but there are better ways to make your videos. This all starts with a good quality camcorder. You do not need a professional digital camera to shoot your vlog videos. When your vlog is successful and you are generating revenue then go and get a pro camera. Until then just use a good quality camcorder that will shoot in HD. If you are going to shoot videos indoors then you need to think about lighting. Shoot some test footage to see how good the lighting is. Invest in some lights if you need to. It is pointless spending out for a high quality camcorder if the lighting is poor.

You need a good quality microphone as well. If you create videos with poor audio quality then you will not succeed with your vlog. For indoor recording get a high quality USB microphone. What about screen recording and video editing? If you are going to create tutorials then you may want to record your computer screen. Desktop recording is easy with Camtasia but this will cost around $200. There is a free option which is CamStudio.

Give this a try first. CamStudio will only work on Windows based computers. If you have a Mac then you can try macOS Mojave. There are other free screen recording applications for Macs. After shooting your video you will need to edit it to make it the best it can be. If you have CamStudio or Camtasia then both of these will do a good job. There are free video editing applications available for Windows and Mac users. Windows Movie Maker is a good video editing suite for Windows users and if you own a Mac then use iMovie. You will find both of these applications easy to use and you can add transitions and other features to make your videos look really great.

Creating your Video

Speak with passion in your voice. Don't be monotone and boring. This will drive people away faster than you can imagine. Be enthusiastic throughout the video. You can't expect your audience to be enthusiastic about your videos if you are not.

If you are creating a tutorial then provide proof that your methods really work. Show them before and after or the end result whatever applies. If other people use your methods then ask them to provide a video testimonial. Add as much social proof as you   can.

Appeal to people's emotions as much as possible in your video. Tell them how exciting it will be for them to travel to the destination you are filming in. Or tell them how beautiful they will look after using your make up tips.

Test how well your Videos are received

In your mind you have created a great video but what really counts is what your audience thinks. You need to look at a few things here such as how many viewers watched your video from beginning to end? If that wasn't the case for a lot of viewers at what stage of the video did they stop watching it? Is there a problem with a certain section of the video? How many people liked the video and how many gave it a "thumbs down"? Read through the comments and see if there are any criticisms there. Don't take them personally. Treat them as good feedback to create better videos in the future. What can you do if your video was not well received? Well you can either edit it to add the information that people in the comments say was missing, or you can create a new video that covers this. So now you know how to create great videos that will keep people engaged and wanting more from your vlog. Go with the majority flow. With all videos there will always be someone that has a complaint to make. If the majority of viewers like your video then you are on the right track. Always ask viewers of your videos to subscribe to your channel if they haven't already. Ask them to "like" the video as well and encourage them to leave comments so that you can create better videos in the future. Tell your viewers that your vlog is for them so any feedback is very helpful. Do everything that you can to appeal to people's emotions. Tell them that they can do whatever you are showing them to do. Use words like "exciting", "fantastic" and other superlatives. And always be passionate in your videos!

Chapter 16: optimizing your youtube videos

Optimizing your videos properly is essential. When you are first starting out this is really important as you need to do everything that you can to ensure that your videos come up in a YouTube search. It will also increase your chances of your videos ranking high in Google as well.

It all starts with Keyword Research

You need to find out what people are likely to enter into the search box in YouTube to find your videos. The best way to do this is through keyword research. You can do this for free using the Google Keyword Planner. You will need to create a free Google Adwords account to access this tool. Let's say that you are creating a video about travelling to Japan. When you are in the Google Keyword Planner enter the seed keyword "Japan Travel" and then see what other keyword suggestions Google has to offer. You can download these suggestions in a CSV file which you can open with most spreadsheet applications such as Microsoft Excel. Go through the list and choose the best keywords. Look at the estimated search volumes. You want to come up with a list of around 10 keywords for each video. Decide which keyword will be your "main" keyword. Maybe this could be "travel to Japan".

Create a Compelling Title around your Main Keyword

You need to come up with an appealing title so that when people see your video in the search results they will want to watch it. So for our Japan example you could use something like "Travel To Japan For Fun And Excitement". Make sure that you include your main keyword in the title. Don't just leave the title as "Travel To Japan". This will not inspire that many people to watch your video. Use other words to create excitement. Another approach may be "Travel To Japan – You Won't Believe What Happened To Me!" This creates curiosity. Try writing a number of different titles with your keyword in them. Go for 10 different titles and then choose the best one. If you can get the keyword in at the beginning of the title then this is preferable but it doesn't matter that much. So just go wild here with your ideas. Remember that the more enticing you make your title the more views you will get.

Write a Keyword Rich Description

Some people like to read the description of a video before they watch it so make this compelling as well. We recommend that your description is at least 300 words long and contains your secondary keywords that you found earlier. Tell people what the video is about but don't give everything away. You can always say something like "you won't believe what happened at the end of this video" or "I have a big surprise for you at the end of the video". Just use techniques to hook the viewer and encourage them to watch all the way through. Don't go crazy with keywords in the description. If you can't fit them in naturally then don't add them.

Use the Right Tags for your Video

Only use keywords in tags that are related to your video. If your video is about travelling to Japan then don't add unrelated keywords in such as "how to speak Chinese". If someone is looking to learn Chinese and watches your video they will be very unimpressed that there is nothing about learning Chinese in it. So choose about 5 related keywords (including your main keyword) and add these as tags. There is a 400 character limit on tags with YouTube at the time of writing. This doesn't mean that you have to use every last character.

Be sure to Speak your Main Keywords in the Video

This one might surprise you. The thing is that technology has really advanced over the last few years and YouTube can understand English (and maybe other languages) so it will pick up on certain key phrases.

Nobody knows just how accurate the YouTube system is for recognizing spoken keywords but estimates suggest as high as 80%. This will continually improve so it is really worth mentioning your main keyword and some secondary keywords in your video. Be sure to plan for this when creating your video script.

Good Video Optimization doesn't take long

If you have spent a great deal of time creating a video script and a story board as we suggested then it seems crazy not to spend a few minutes optimizing your videos so that they have the maximum chance of being found in a search. So use these video optimization tips every time. Don't skip the keyword research step as this is the most important task. It will not take you long to uncover some good keywords. Even if you have a large following with your vlog we would always recommend that you optimize each video.

Chapter 17: promoting your vlog

When you create your new vlog and start to upload your videos you must do more than just rely on the optimization tactics we discussed in the last chapter for search traffic. You need to tell the world about your   new   vlog!

It is never a case of "build it and they will come". You need to put in some continuous promotional effort to give your vlog every chance of developing a large following. Some vloggers wait until they have a number of videos on their vlog such as 10 to 30, but our advice is to start promoting your blog as soon as your first video   is   up.

If you don't have a huge social media following at the moment then don't let that stop you. Some vloggers started off with social accounts of less than 50 followers and now they are doing very well. The key thing is to be consistent.

Tell Everyone that you know

Make a list of all of your family members, friends, work colleagues past and present and any other people that you know. Use Facebook, email and any other means that you have to contact them and tell them about your new vlog. If you haven't spoken to some of these people in years then write them a nice email and tell them that you miss them. Ask them to get in touch with you again if you want to do that. Then tell them that you have started a new vlog and that you would really appreciate their support. This is something that is so easy to do but most people don't do it. Unless you have a very good reason for not telling the people you already know about your vlog then tell them! It can be a lot of fun making contact with people you have not been in touch with for years. Ask them to spread the word to the people that they know too.

Use Reddit

If you don't have a Reddit account then sign up for one today. It is a very popular platform that is overlooked by most people. People create Sub Reddits on the platform that are dedicated to specific subjects and niches. Not all of these are going to be a hit for you but here are some good ones for new vloggers:

- /r/NewTubers

- /r/vlog
- /r/vlogs
- /r/vlogger

- /r/vlogging

Once you get your Reddit account use it to comment on other peoples accounts. Try to create an account that matches your vlog brand name. Be sure to follow the rules on Reddit as you can get your account closed very quickly if they think you are spamming. Take a look at what others do in the Sub Reddits mentioned above.

Use Facebook

You cannot and mustn't ignore the biggest social media platform. Facebook is a great place for posting videos and getting people to share your content. Create a Facebook Page around your vlog brand. It is really easy to do and there are plenty of videos on YouTube to show you how to do this effectively. Add branded artwork to your Facebook page. Make it look really professional. Be sure to post other useful content on your page as well as your vlog videos. Become friends with other people on Facebook that are in your niche. Look for Facebook Groups that you can join that are related too. Facebook has a good advertising service where you can specifically target your audience to drive traffic to your Facebook Page. It is not just about getting "likes" to your page. Encourage people to share and leave comments as well.

Use Twitter

Twitter is a huge social media platform that it can be difficult to have success with. But it is worth making the effort because with a large Twitter following you can really drive up subscriptions to your vlog.

 Again don't just make tweets about your vlog videos. If this is all that you do then people will stop responding to your tweets. Post some other useful tweets and re-tweet content from other Twitter users that is relevant to your vlog. Succeeding with Twitter (as with other social platforms) is all about reaching out to others. Follow people that you believe have an interest in your niche and reply to the tweets that they make and retweet them. Share their content as much as you can.

Use Instagram

A lot of people shy away from Instagram because it can be tricky to gain a following there. But it is really worth persisting with as you can get a lot of YouTube views from this platform. Instagram users like images as well as videos. So take an interesting screenshot from your vlog videos and post this asking people to check it out. One thing you need to know about Instagram is that you can't link directly to your YouTube vlog from posts. They do not allow external links. So you need to set up a good bio in Instagram and link to your vlog from there. When you make a post tell people that the link to your vlog is in your bio. It is always a good idea to tell people exactly what you want them to do.

Use Quora

Quora.com is a forum where questions are asked on just about every topic under the sun. It has a huge user base and is often overlooked as a promotional tool for vloggers. It is also a great place to get inspiration for future videos for your vlog. Find questions that have a direct relation to videos on your vlog. Write an answer and then add something like "for a more detailed answer to this question please take a look at this video". If your video does a really good job answering the question then it will receive a lot of "up votes" which means more and more Quora users will watch it.

Make Comments on Videos posted by popular YouTubers'

While it is true that there are a lot of morons that make stupid comments on most YouTube videos (you will have to deal with this yourself at some stage) there are actually a lot of genuine people that leave comments as well. Your job is to become one of these genuine people that leave sensible comments. Find other related videos in your niche and leave a positive comment about it. By becoming part of the conversation and adding value to other people's videos there is a good chance that they will reciprocate by clicking on your username and checking out your channel.

This is one of the easiest and most effective ways to get more video views and subscribers so make sure that you do this. It is very important that you choose the videos of popular YouTubers' that have some relation to your vlog. You don't have to just add constructive comments to popular videos either. Find other related high quality videos that don't have as many views and add comments to those too. Don't use a spam approach here – never ask the video poster to check out your channel and subscribe.

Use the YTTalk Forum

Join the YTTalk forum. It is a very active forum for the YouTube community and there are people there with small and large channels. Start contributing to other people's posts and then use the forum as a feedback mechanism for your videos. People that post videos on YouTube tend to watch other people's videos as well so this is a great place to find more viewers and subscribers. As always look to add value with your posts and replies. Don't resort to any form of spam.

Use Empire.Kred

Most vlog owners have never even heard of Empire.Kred let alone use it. When you sign up you are awarded a stock value based on your social influence. You can post your vlog content here and persuade other influencers on the platform to check it out and engage with it. Other influencers on Empire.Kred can purchase stock in you if they like what you are doing. This will increase the amount of "eaves" that you have (the digital currency used). You can use your eaves to create specific tasks such as requesting other influencers to view your latest video etc. You are not allowed to ask for specific engagement activities such as sharing, commenting or liking. Just leave it to the influencer to make their own decision on this. Influencers will earn eaves from you for completing the task. If the influencers like your vlog they will subscribe to your channel.

Engage with all Comments you receive

The best way to promote your vlog is to create a community. As you grow your community more and more people will come back to your videos and share them, like them and leave comments. You need to monitor comments on all of your videos and respond to them as fast as you can. People will really appreciate that you took the time to respond to their comments. You are proving that you are a real person and care about what they have to say. This will motivate them to subscribe if they haven't already done so and keep an eye out for your future videos.

Chapter 18: free tools for growing your youtube Channel

There are some essential tools that you can use to grow your YouTube channel and the good news is that they are all free. Most of them are easy to use and the benefits are pretty obvious. Let's take a look at some of the best free tools.

TubeBuddy

The major benefit of using TubeBuddy is that it will save you a lot of time. It also provides you with some great pointers to really grow your YouTube channel. TubeBuddy is a browser app which works with the most commonly used browsers such as Google Chrome, Mozilla Firefox and Safari. When you use TubeBuddy you will find that it has dozens of useful features from checking the SEO optimization of your videos to helping you promote your channel. There are comprehensive training videos available that explain everything really well. You can literally save hours each week with this app.

You can do a great deal with the free version of TubeBuddy and we suggest that you start with this. If you want more features then there is a Pro package available for $9 a month, a Star package for $19 a month and a Legend package for $49 a month.

YouTube Creator Studio

This is another free app which is great for checking the performance of your channel and videos on the go. You can use it on your iPhone by downloading it here and your Android phone by downloading here. You can't actually manage your videos with this app but you can do everything else. It is great for finding out just how well your videos are performing, as well as look at the overall performance of your channel wherever you are. There is a filter feature where you can respond to comments and create that essential connection with your viewers. This feature alone makes the app worth installing on your smartphone.

Buffer.com

We explained to you in the previous chapter that using social media to grow your YouTube channel and vlog is highly recommended. To help you share your videos on social media platforms the Buffer app is a really great tool. With Buffer you can schedule and post your content on Facebook, Twitter, Instagram, Pinterest and LinkedIn. There is one simple dashboard for managing everything. The free Buffer plan is for a maximum of 3 social accounts and you can schedule 10 posts a month as a single user. If you have more than 3 social accounts or plan to make more than 10 posts a month then there are premium plans you can go for starting at $15 a month. Whatever plan you choose you will save a lot of time if you use Buffer to schedule your posts. There is a browser extension that you can use to post content automatically to Facebook, Twitter and Pinterest.

Audio Hero

It can be a real challenge to find great royalty free music for your YouTube videos. Audio Hero makes finding great music and sound effects for your videos really easy. There is a huge library of more than 250,000 music clips and sound effects to choose from so you should never have any difficulty finding what you want. Although the Audio Hero app is free, to use the sound tracks you will have to pay a small fee. This is a lot better than running the risk of infringing copyright and even having your videos removed. At the time of writing you can purchase 50 downloads of royalty free music clips or sound effects for only $9.99.

Snappa

Creating your own graphics or finding a good and reliable graphic designer can be a real headache. You know that you need high quality graphics to grow your YouTube channel so what do you do? Just use Snappa of course! There are a lot of premade templates you can use in Snappa. You can use Snappa easily to create your initial channel art and then for really attractive video thumbnails as you upload your videos. It is really important that your thumbnails look great. This can literally mean the difference between somebody watching your video and someone else's. The free version has 5,000 templates and you can create 5 graphics a month. If you want more then plans start at $10 a month.

Repost for Instagram

Repost for Instagram is another useful app for your iPhone or Android phone. Get the Android version here and the iPhone version here. We cannot recommend Instagram highly enough as a great social platform to promote your vlog. It has a huge user base that is growing all the time. When you have the Repost for Instagram app you will be able to repost videos or images that your followers shared. You can actually include the username of the person that shared the content (highly recommended) so that they get credit and your followers can easily check them out.

Chapter 19: ways to monetize your vlog

OK so you have your YouTube channel set up correctly, you have uploaded some vlog videos and you are working hard to increase your subscriber numbers and video views. Where is the reward for all of this?

This guide is about vlogging for profit so we are going to share with you some of the best ways to monetize your vlog here. The truth is that there are many different ways that you can monetize your vlog and videos.

YouTube Partner

When you become a YouTube Partner you can display Google Adsense ads on videos that you choose. If you are not aware of Google Adsense it is used by content publishers (such as vloggers and blog owners) to display Google Ads in or on their content. Every time an ad is clicked you share the revenue with YouTube. Now the first thing to say here is that it is unlikely that you will make a life changing income with Google Adsense on your videos even if you have millions of views. There are also various factors which affect how much of the revenue you receive such as:

• The number of views an ad receives (not all viewers of your video will see the ad)
• The length of time that the ad was visible (some ads are actually short videos)
• Was there any interaction with the ad?
• The demographics of your audience
• The amount of advertisers that want to advertise in your niche at the current time

As you have probably worked out it is not easy to predict the money you will make by enabling Google Adsense on your videos. But you don't have to worry about any of the factors above other than trying to get as many views to your video as possible.

There are different types of Google Adsense ads that you can display on your videos. One of the most common is a standard banner displaying at the bottom of the video. There are also short video trailers that can display at the start, during your video or at the end. Sometimes the viewer can skip these trailers and other times they will have to watch them. You will need to meet a number of criteria to be eligible for the YouTube Partner program and displaying Google Adsense ads. The rules change often so it is best to visit

https://support.google.com/youtube/ans wer/72851#eligibility to see what the latest rules are. Once you are a confirmed partner it is easy to monetize any of your videos by logging into your YouTube account and enabling monetization. There are a number of payment methods that you can choose from including a check, wire transfer, electronic funds transfer, Western Union and more. You need to think carefully about enabling these ads on your videos. Some viewers will not mind an Adsense banner at the bottom of the video. A trailer at the start that cannot be skipped may test the patience of some viewers though especially if they are new to your vlog.

Affiliate Marketing

With affiliate marketing you promote other people's products and when a sale is made you earn a commission. Commissions range from very small (a few cents) to very large (hundreds of dollars) for high ticket items. Videos are a lot more persuasive than written text so you could be demonstrating a product or a piece of software and then add your affiliate link in the description. Some people that own makeup vlogs for example make a fortune every month through affiliate marketing. With most vlog niches there will be affiliate products and services that you can promote. You just need to find them. Use Google or another search engine and type in the type of product or service and then "affiliate program". So an example would be "makeup affiliate program". You can promote physical products and digital products too. Digital products

177

would normally be software, a "how to" guide, training videos and so on. It can be harder to make a sale with digital products but the commissions are usually a lot higher than with physical products.

Merchandising

You can create your own merchandising for your vlog brand. A good example of this is a t-shirt or sweatshirt with your brand logo on it or even caps. There are companies you can use that will supply the clothes or caps in the right sizes and colors with your design printed on them. There are other merchandising goods that are somewhat easier then clothes such as USB memory sticks with your logo, calendars with your logo, pens with your logo, phone cases and much more. It is easy to find a company that will brand popular items for you. Merchandising is not something that you need to think about when you are first starting out with your vlog. You will need a lot of active subscribers to make a profit from merchandising. But once you reach that large subscriber base then you can sell a lot of merchandise items regular and make good money.

Selling your own Products/Services

This is something that you can do fairly quickly with your vlog. There are many different products and services that you can sell from your vlog. Here are some examples:

- A   book
- A   "how   to"   guide
- A   video   training   course
- Coaching   services

The best way to do this is to teach your audience the basics of achieving something and then tell them that if they want to know the real advanced methods then they need your product. Provide value in your videos to get your audience hooked but don't give everything away for free.

Chapter 20: vlogging best practices

If you want your vlog to be successful there are a few best practices that we highly recommend that you adopt. These best practices are followed by all successful vloggers so you need to pay close attention here and follow them too.

Always Create High Quality Videos

Always put your audience first. What are they looking for? What answers do they need to solve problems in their life? How can you make their life more exciting and how can you entertain your audience? Never upload low quality videos to your vlog because you feel under pressure to give your audience something. It is always about quality and not quantity. If you put out something low quality then you will lose your audience. Just don't do this! Use good equipment and software to create your videos. You don't need the most expensive digital camera on the market, but you do need to create videos that are clear with good audio quality. Never use a poor quality microphone.

180

Always be passionate and excited in your videos. If you are not passionate how can you expect your audience to be?

Consistency

Once you start putting out your high quality videos then your audience will want more and more from you. You need to be consistent and create videos to a schedule of some kind. If you leave it too long between one video and the next you will   lose   people. You need to be patient with your vlog. OK some vlogs have taken off really quickly and made their owners a lot of money in record time. But this is the exception rather than the rule. Take your time and be patient and focus on being consistent with quality and posting schedules.

Focus on getting more Subscribers

Don't focus on money focus on gaining new subscribers. Do everything you can to get the word out about your vlog. When the subscribers come so will the money.

Use social media extensively and try other methods to promote your vlog.

Know what is working

YouTube has a lot of analytics to help you work out which of your videos are performing the best. So use this to discover what is working and what is not. Do more of what is working! Tweak things to make them better. Check your videos for the correct optimization.

Conclusion

There has never ever been a greater time to begin a vlog, and I have offered you all that you require within this book to plan and execute effectively. The need for premium vlogs is going to keep on increasing so enter now to use the increasing trend. Videos will constantly be the favored medium for Web users. Individuals slouch and if they can devote 5 minutes to see a video on how to perform something, this is a lot simpler than investing 20 minutes going through a 5,000-word article. With a vlog, you have a terrific chance to engage with your audience.

Ask them questions within your videos and ask that they leave you responses in the comments area. You could, after that, thank them by responding to their comments. You want to do every little thing which you could to expand your vlog.

This is going to boost your capacity to generate income from it. So make certain to optimize all of your videos correctly and keep getting the word out on social networks. So now it is over to you. Begin arranging your brand-new vlog today. If you have to purchase some top quality recording tools, then do so. It is going to definitely be worth it, and it will reinforce your dedication to your vlog. I wish you excellence with your vlog!

Printed in the USA
CPSIA information can be obtained
at www.ICGtesting.com
LVHW010713171023
761330LV00005B/74